I0500384

NATIONAL INCIDENT MANAGEMENT SYSTEM

Guideline for the Credentialing of Personnel

August 2011

August 2011

OVERVIEW

PURPOSE

The Department of Homeland Security (DHS)/Federal Emergency Management Agency (FEMA) developed the National Incident Management System (NIMS) Guideline for the Credentialing of Personnel (the guideline) to describe national credentialing standards and to provide written guidance regarding the use of those standards. This document describes credentialing and typing processes and identifies tools which Federal Emergency Response Officials (FERO) and emergency managers at all levels of government may use both routinely and to facilitate multijurisdictional coordinated responses. Through this guideline, DHS/FEMA encourages interoperability among Federal, State, local, territorial, tribal, and private sector officials in order to facilitate emergency responder deployment for response, recovery, and restoration. This guideline also provides information about where emergency response leaders can obtain expertise and technical assistance in using the national standards or in ways they can adapt the standards to department, agency, jurisdiction, or organization needs.

APPLICABILITY

Each Federal agency with responsibilities under the National Response Framework is required to ensure that incident management personnel, emergency response providers, and other personnel (including temporary personnel) and resources likely needed to respond to a natural disaster, act of terrorism, or other manmade disaster are credentialed and typed in accordance with 6 U.S.C. § 320. In addition, Homeland Security Presidential Directive – 5 (HSPD -5), *Management of Domestic Incidents*, requires that the heads of Federal departments and agencies adopt the National Incident Management System. DHS interprets these authorities to require agencies to ensure that their personnel are credentialed and typed according to these guidelines. Federal Legislative and Judicial Branches, State, local, tribal, private sector partners, and non-governmental organizations (NGO) are not required to credential their personnel in accordance with these guidelines. These non-Federal entities do not need to comply with the Federal Information Processing Standards (FIPS) 201, an open technical standard used by Federal officials for uniform credentialing and access control or other Federal identification requirements for emergency response purposes. However, DHS/FEMA strongly encourages them to do so, in order to leverage the Federal investment in the FIPS 201 infrastructure and facilitating interoperability for personnel deployed outside their home jurisdiction.

INTENDED AUDIENCE

This document, developed and maintained by DHS/FEMA, is written for government executives; emergency management practitioners; private-sector, volunteer, and NGO leaders; and critical infrastructure (CI) owners and operators. It is addressed to senior elected and appointed leaders, such as Federal department and/or agency heads, State governors, mayors, tribal leaders, and city

1

and/or county officials who have a responsibility to provide effective response. It also is intended for use by private-sector entities entering an impacted area to carry out their own response and recovery activities within the Incident Command System (ICS). For these users, this guideline is augmented with online access to supporting documents, further training, and an evolving resource for exchanging lessons learned.

SCOPE

This guideline applies to incidents such as large-scale terrorist attacks or catastrophic natural disasters where mutual aid and multijurisdictional aid is required. It can be useful for international cross-border initiatives undertaken by States and tribes.

NIMS OVERVIEW

Mandated by Homeland Security Presidential Directive 5 (HSPD-5), *Management of Domestic Incidents*, and as outlined in the National Incident Management System (NIMS) FEMA P-501, NIMS provides a consistent nationwide template to enable Federal, State, tribal, and local governments, NGOs, and the private sector to work together to prevent, protect against, respond to, recover from, and mitigate the effects of incidents, regardless of cause, size, location, or complexity. NIMS represents a core set of doctrines, concepts, principles, terminology, and organizational processes that enables effective, efficient, and collaborative incident management. This consistency provides the foundation for utilization of NIMS for all incidents, ranging from daily occurrences to incidents requiring a coordinated Federal response.

The NIMS documents integrate best practices into a comprehensive framework for use by emergency management and response personnel in an all-hazards context nationwide. HSPD-5 requires all Federal departments and agencies to adopt NIMS and to use it in their individual incident management programs and activities, as well as in support of all actions taken to assist State, local, and tribal governments. State, local, and tribal governments are not required to participate in NIMS or adopt these best practices. As applied to non-Federal entities, the NIMS documents contain guidance that is not legally binding. However, in order to participate in NIMS and to be considered NIMS compliant, it is necessary for entities to adhere to the standards, practices, and/or minimum criteria presented in the NIMS guidance documents. It is also important to note that although State, local, and tribal governments and NGOs are not required to adhere to NIMS Guidelines, HSPD-5 requires Federal departments and agencies to make adoption of NIMS by State, local, and tribal governments and NGOs a condition for Federal preparedness assistance through grants, contracts, and other activities.

A basic premise of NIMS is that all incidents begin and end locally. The Federal Government supports State, local, and tribal authorities when their resources are overwhelmed or anticipated to be overwhelmed. The intention of the Federal Government in these situations is not to command the response, but rather to support the affected State, local, and tribal authorities. This is most easily achieved when all the entities are participating in a unified system of emergency management and incident response. NIMS also recognizes the role that NGOs and the private sector have in preparedness and activities to prevent, protect against, respond to, recover from, and mitigate the effects of incidents. To ensure unity of effort, NIMS advocates standards to include training, experience, credentialing, validation, and physical and medical fitness. Federal, State, tribal, and local certifying agencies, and professional and private organizations with personnel involved in emergency management and incident response, are encouraged to credential those individuals in their respective disciplines or jurisdictions.

DEFINITION OF CREDENTIALING

As the basis for this document, DHS/FEMA refers to the definition of credentialing provided by the Homeland Security Act of 2002, as amended by the Implementing Recommendations of the 9/11 Commission Act of 2007. This language, codified in 6 United States Code (U.S.C.) § 311, provides that:

> *"The terms 'credentialed' and 'credentialing' mean having provided, or providing, respectively, documentation that identifies personnel and authenticates and verifies the qualifications of such personnel by ensuring that such personnel possess a minimum common level of training, experience, physical and medical fitness, and capability appropriate for a particular position..."*

FEMA ADMINISTRATOR'S RESPONSIBILITIES

Per 6 U.S.C. § 320, the FEMA Administrator is responsible for ensuring the development and implementation of credentialing of emergency response providers.

> *"The Administrator shall enter into a memorandum of understanding with the administrators of the Emergency Management Assistance Compact (EMAC), State, local, and tribal governments, and organizations that represent emergency response providers, to collaborate on developing standards for deployment capabilities, including for credentialing and typing of incident management personnel, emergency response providers, and other personnel (including temporary personnel) and resources likely needed to respond to natural disasters, acts of terrorism, and other man-made disasters."*

Section 320 of title 6, U.S.C., also calls on the Administrator to "provide standards" and "detailed written guidance" to:

> *"Each Federal agency that has responsibilities under the National Response Plan[1] to aid that agency with credentialing and typing incident management personnel, emergency response providers, and other personnel (including temporary personnel) and resources likely needed to respond to a natural disaster, act of terrorism, or other man-made disaster; and*
>
> *State, local, and tribal governments, to aid such governments with credentialing and typing of State, local, and tribal incident management personnel, emergency response*

---

[1] The National Response Framework superseded the National Response Plan.

*providers, and other personnel (including temporary personnel) and resources likely
needed to respond to a natural disaster, act of terrorism, or other man-made disaster."*

In addition, 6 U.S.C. § 320 requires the FEMA Administrator to provide expertise and technical
assistance to:

*"aid Federal, State, local, and tribal government agencies with credentialing and
typing incident management personnel, emergency response providers, and other
personnel (including temporary personnel) and resources likely needed to
respond to a natural disaster, act of terrorism, or other man-made disaster."*

SECTION 1 - NATIONAL CREDENTIALING STANDARDS

GENERAL INFORMATION

Credentialing is essential to the emergency management community in that it ensures and validates the identity and attributes (e.g., affiliations, skills, or privileges) of individuals or members of response teams through standards. Having established standards allows the community to plan for, request, and have confidence in resources deployed from other jurisdictions for emergency assistance. Credentialing ensures that personnel resources match requests, and it supports effective management of deployed responders. This guideline provides information useful to all response organizations. It includes operational definitions, important terms, and descriptions of credentialing processes.

DHS/FEMA is committed to improving emergency management and response capabilities in the United States for all major disasters and other incidents where mutual aid is required. DHS/FEMA recognizes the existing authority for States and tribes to regulate mutual aid within their borders. The intent is to build on existing processes and systems to improve the delivery of interstate mutual aid. This guideline does not preempt or diminish the sovereignty of the States and tribes to manage routine and/or local response operations in accordance with their laws.

The process of credentialing and affiliation already exists in many jurisdictions, including in some States that have a "just in time" credentialing procedure at the time of deployment. Nothing in this guideline should be construed as preempting States from executing either standard or just-in-time credentialing.

EXPERTISE AND TECHNICAL ASSISTANCE

FEMA provides credentialing expertise and technical assistance to any Federal, State, tribal or local department, agency, jurisdiction, or organization with emergency management responsibilities. The National Integration Center (NIC), part of FEMA's National Preparedness Directorate, is the executive agent for providing this expertise and assistance.

The NIC provides online support for credentialing and other NIMS-related issues through the NIMS Support Center that can be accessed on the Internet at http://www.fema.gov/emergency/nims/.

Questions regarding the credentialing process should be directed to FEMA-NIMS@dhs.gov or 202-646-3850.

In addition, each FEMA Region has a NIMS Coordinator available to answer questions and provide technical assistance. A list of these coordinators is located on the Internet at http://www.fema.gov/emergency/nims/NIMScoordinators.shtm.

IDENTIFICATION, QUALIFICATION, AND TYPING

Identification, Qualification, and Typing are the key elements of the guideline. As defined in law, credentialing involves providing documentation that communicates and authenticates identity, as well as verifies the holder's qualifications as an emergency responder. The law also calls for typing of incident management personnel, emergency response providers, and other personnel (including temporary personnel) and resources needed for emergency response. The following sections describe these elements.

IDENTIFICATION

The guideline for verifying Non-Federal personal identity of emergency management and response personnel is based on the Federal Chief Information Officers (CIO) Council's May 2009 guidance, "Personal Identity Verification Interoperability for Non-Federal Issuers.[2]"

The guidelines seek to leverage the Federal Government's investments in creating a credentialing infrastructure so that non-Federal entities can achieve interoperability more economically and efficiently. U.S. policy is to enhance security, increase efficiency, reduce identity fraud, and protect personal privacy by establishing a mandatory standard for secure and reliable forms of credentials issued by the Executive Branch of the Federal Government to its employees and contractors (including contractor employees). The Federal Government credential is known as a Personal Identity Verification (PIV) card.

A credential issued by a non-Federal authority that is designed to be interoperable with the Federal PIV credential is known as a PIV-Interoperable (PIV-I) card. Both PIV and PIV-I use the same open technical standard: Federal Information Processing Standards (FIPS) 201. The difference between PIV and PIV-I is that the PIV includes a type of background check that is unique to Federal employees and contractors.

The PIV/PIV-I solution is recommended because it resolves the four core process and technical barriers to establishing interoperability in identification and access control systems:

- Common terminology;

- Technical requirements for how identity cards/media interact with controlling infrastructure;

- A system of unique identifiers that allow individuals and organizations to be recognized across all identity cards/ media; and

- Processes that allow issuance that support the requisite level of trust in the identity of the holder, as well as attributes and privileges where applicable.

---

[2] Refer to www.cio.gov to obtain a copy http://www.cio.gov/documents_details.cfm/uid/1F4376A0-2170-9AD7-F2D502311E4D26E9/structure/Information%20Technology/category/HSPD-12

Required Federal Compliance

In accordance with HSPD-12, *Policy for a Common Identification Standard for Federal Employees and Contractors*, and FIPS 201, Federal departments and agencies must identify their personnel who are likely to be deployed in accordance with assignments in the National Response Framework (NRF), National Infrastructure Protection Plan (NIPP), or National Continuity Policy Implementation Plan (NCPIP).[3] These personnel will be designated as FEROs, and their FIPS 201 credentials visually marked accordingly. Additionally, non-Federal personnel assigned to work in Federal offices will be credentialed in accordance with FIPS 201.

Sample of Federal Information Processing Standards 201 Identification Card

DHS advocates the use of FIPS 201, PIV-I, and other permanent identity cards that support secure, electronic, real-time identity verification and authentication at very high levels of assurance. Key elements of this card are shown in Figure 1 below.

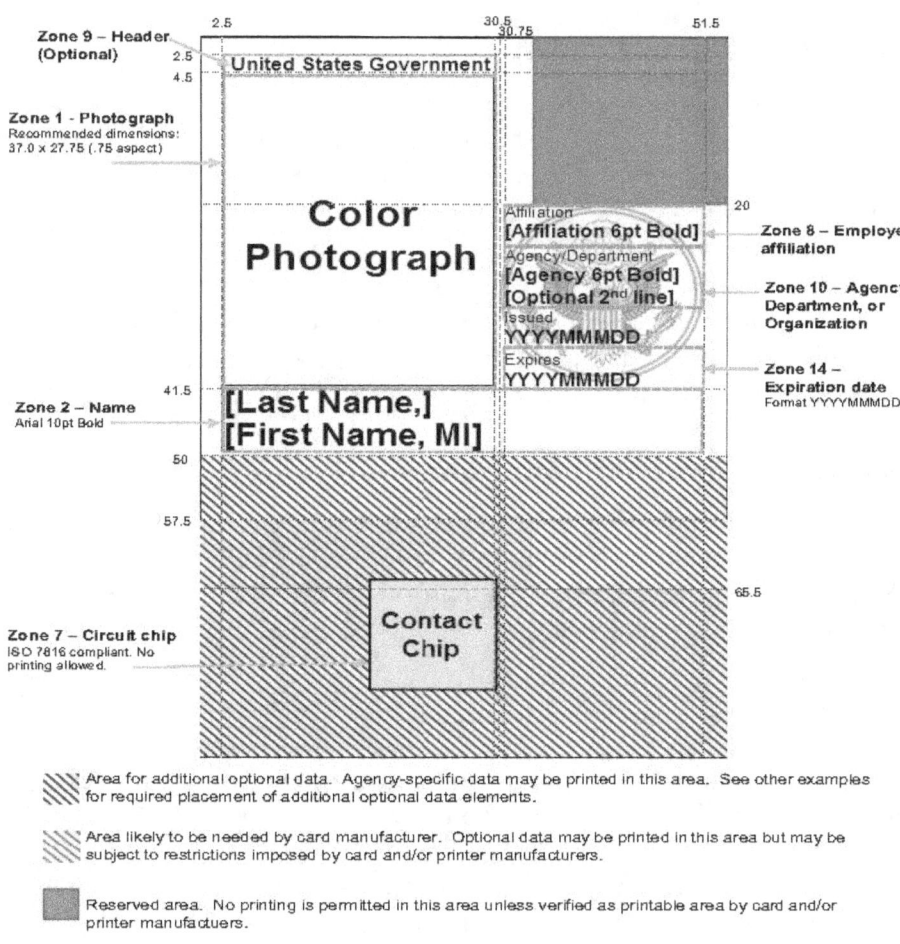

Figure 1: Example Format of FIPS 201 Card

---

[3] Federal agencies are responsible for applying agency-specific inventory and qualification processes. This requirement is found in 6 U.S.C. 751.

Federal employee PIV credentials are one example of approved identification cards. Others under the guideline include the U.S. General Services Administration (GSA) approved PIV-I/First Responder Authentication Credentials (PIV-I/FRAC), the Department of Defense's Common Access Card (CAC), and private sector-issued GSA approved PIV-I employee credentials.

Non-Federal Government Identification Alternatives

State, local, and tribal jurisdictions are encouraged to use the Federal CIO's PIV-I guidance to develop credentials similar to the Federal Government's PIV cards to promote consistency. If using a similar format, non-Federal issuers are encouraged to fill Zone 9-Header with the State, local, tribal government, private sector, or volunteer or not-for-profit organization as appropriate. Additionally, the image underlying Zones 8, 10, and 14 would be the emblem for their organization. Additional optional placements of data are contained in FIPS 201 itself which can be obtained from National Institute of Standards and Technology (http://csrc.nist.gov/).

Public/Private Sector Interoperability

To support issues of "trust" between public and private-sector issued identity credentials, the Federal Government has published PIV-I. The guidance advocates a set of minimum technical and process requirements to support uniform acceptance and trust of non-Federally issued identity cards or documents. PIV-I details solutions to the four interoperability barriers (previously described in this section) that currently preclude higher levels of trust of non-Federally issued identity cards. If followed, the PIV-I guidance provides a supporting framework for technical interoperability with the nearly 10 million Federally credentialed uniformed and civilian employees and contractors. It supports enhanced integration and reduced costs in day-to-day operations as well as during response and incident management.

Non PIV-I Options

To achieve an interoperable and consistent national system, State, local and tribal governments are encouraged, to the maximum degree possible, to follow the Federal standard FIPS 201/HSPD-12 and GSA approved PIV-I. When this is not possible, non PIV-I organizations are asked to issue identification that matches, as closely as possible, the format of PIV-I cards.

QUALIFICATION

Personnel qualifications (education, training, experience, and certification/licensure and medical/physical fitness for deployment) are typically position specific. Determining essential functions, levels of training, experience levels, required licensure and certifications, and physical and medical fitness for a position should be part of a job-task analysis. This analysis normally incorporates, as appropriate, input from job incumbents, managers, industry organizations, and others with knowledge of the position requirements. Departments, agencies, and authorities having jurisdiction over positions are responsible for determining position requirements through a job-task analysis process.

Any person credentialed and authorized for deployment through Emergency Management Assistance Compact (EMAC) is qualified to serve in the role for which he or she is deployed.

NIMS guidance on credentialing, NIMS Guide 0002 (*National Credentialing Definition and Criteria*) and this guideline, refers to the identification and qualification information a person will present to the requesting jurisdiction. NIMS guidance on credentialing does not confer the authority or privilege to practice any profession. For responders not deployed through EMAC only the receiving department, agency, or jurisdiction can extend that privilege or authority after evaluating the person's information.

Two key elements in the qualification process include typing personnel and resources and certifying that personnel in fact possesses at least the minimum level of training, experience, licensure, certification, and fitness to perform the job.

Typing

As noted in NIMS, type refers to the level of resource capability. Typing (categorizing, by capability, the resources requested, deployed, and used in incidents) provides managers with additional information to aid in the selection and best use of resources likely needed to respond to natural disasters, acts of terrorism, and other manmade disasters (6 U.S.C. § 320(a)). The type assigned to a resource or a component is based on a minimum level of capability described by the identified measure(s) for that resource. This provision requires the identification of specific positions and job titles of responding personnel. Typing requires development of standards for qualifying for these positions and job titles.

The qualifications of employees under the credentialing program shall be determined by their department, agency, or jurisdiction, based on the functions and missions these personnel will perform. For Federal employees, the determination typically relates to assignments under one of the following.

- The NRF Emergency Support Function (ESF) under which they will operate;
- The sector(s) of the NIPP they will support; and/or
- Their national essential functions as government officials.

The guideline supplements the NIMS discipline specific Job Titles that list the minimum education, training, experience, certification, licensure, and medical/physical wellness as qualifications for NIMS credentialed positions. These Job Titles and qualifications are located at www.fema.gov/emergency/nims/ResourceMngmnt.shtm#item3. Figure 2 is an example of a position-specific qualification requirement for a Job Title.

	Medical Supply Coordinator SAMPLE
DESCRIPTION:	The primary focus of the Medical Supply Coordinator is to acquire and maintain control of appropriate medical equipment and supplies for units assigned to the medical group. The Medical Supply Coordinator coordinates with logistics section of ICS to accomplish medical resupply and ensures distribution to EMS treatment and triage units.
EDUCATION:	Completion of State-approved First Responder or Emergency Medical Responder (EMR) program based on NHTSA National Standard Curriculum.
TRAINING	Completion of the following courses/curricula: 1. ICS-100: Introduction to ICS. 2. ICS-200: Basic ICS. 3. IS-700.A: NIMS, An Introduction. 4. IS-800.B: NRF, An Introduction. 5. HazMat Awareness Training or equivalent basic instruction consistent with: • the hazards anticipated to be present, or present at the scene • the probable impact of those hazards, based upon the mission role of the individual • use of the personal protective equipment consistent with "Guidance on Emergency Responder Personal Protective Equipment (PPE) for Response to CBRN Terrorism Incidents," Dept of HHS, Centers for Disease Control and Prevention, National Institute for Occupational Safety and Health (June 2008).
EXPERIENCE:	One to three years of active participation with an EMS-providing entity, organization, or agency.
LICENSING:	Active status of legal authority to function at the minimum of First Responder or EMR granted by a State, the District of Columbia, or U.S. territory.

Figure 2. Sample Typing

Certification

Certification of personnel ensures "… personnel possess a minimum level of training, experience, physical and medical fitness, and capability appropriate for a particular position…" (6 U.S.C. § 311). This provision requires organizations to test and evaluate their personnel against the qualifications established by the typing efforts. Additionally organizations must "…authenticate qualifications…" through a formal process they designate to approve and sign off on personnel qualifications.

OTHER IMPORTANT ACTIVITIES

In addition to the legally mandated requirements of the credentialing effort (6 U.S.C. §§ 311 and 320), there are other aspects that should be addressed in the credentialing process. Under NIMS, these include the authorization to deploy, control of access to an affected area, affiliation of personnel deploying as part of an organization, and revocation of credentials when necessary.

AUTHORIZATION

To avoid self-deployment by responders that could result in a diversion of resources for disaster survivors, some form of authorization is a key aspect of deployment credentialing. Being credentialed with proof of identity and qualification is not sufficient for deploying to a disaster. Deployment authorization should be documented and may take several forms, from mission assignments to deployment orders and travel authorities.

ACCESS

Access to a disaster should be limited to personnel who have been credentialed and authorized to deploy through a formal agreement between the requesting and providing agencies. The agreements can range from automatic mutual aid agreements, EMAC, and mission assignments to Federal agencies to provide Direct Federal Assistance. Personnel that arrive at an incident who have not been credentialed and authorized should be turned away unless the incident/unified command or the jurisdiction having authority establishes rules specific to the incident, disaster, or emergency.

AFFILIATION

Credentialing, resource typing, and mutual aid agreements provide a framework for personnel and resources responding to support the government-led response operations. Restoration of critical infrastructure, which may be owned by government or private entities, also is a key element to an effective response. During certain stages of a disaster, teams of people will be arriving at an incident site that will require access to perform functions that are outside the purview of government-led response operations and who have no requirement to conform to the credentialing and resource typing requirements. Access control provides a process for identifying and providing services for critical infrastructure and other entities that are located in the affected area and a process for including these entities in phased re-entry planning. An affiliation access process provides a control system for State and local officials, while enabling critical infrastructure owners and operators to designate recovery personnel, employees, contractors, and/or equipment to enter an incident area. Access control and affiliation documentation processes will be used by critical infrastructure owners and operators to deploy the personnel and equipment needed to restore their facilities and services within an incident area based on a timeline deemed appropriate by incident command. Since the CI within an incident area normally falls within State and/or local jurisdictions, processes for access control and affiliation documentation should be administered by the States, territories, tribes, or delegated to local authorities.

REVOCATION

An employee's credentials may be revoked under certain circumstances. If a person leaves a position from a department or agency, the credentialing organization must revoke identification cards and remove the individual's name from the list of credentialed employees within 18 hours to comply with FIPS 201 revocation requirements. Likewise, if an employee's qualifications change, his or her credentialing information must also be updated in all applicable databases or records within the same time constraints. A credentialing system must include a process to revoke credentials.

VERIFICATION

In designing a credentialing system, an authority should consider how the credential will be verified. PIV and PIV-I credentials can be electronically read using readily available handheld and stationary devices. The credentialing can also be linked to back end systems that will allow the credentialing authority to manage and update attributes associated with its credentialed holder.

SUMMARY

Implementing credentialing provides confidence that the personnel and resources provided under mutual aid match the request. Credentialing helps ensure that both requester and supplier are using the same criteria to certify personnel. It alleviates one concern from communities already struggling with the effects of a disaster. In order for this system to work, it is imperative that the basic principles of identity, qualification/affiliation, and authorities are embraced and utilized.

Developing a culture of credentialing is also important so that when an event occurs, the response is disciplined and the adverse effects of an unauthorized deployment are avoided.

SECTION 2 – CREDENTIALING OF FEDERAL EMERGENCY RESPONSE OFFICIALS

GENERAL GUIDANCE

This section provides guidance on credentialing and typing of Federal departments and agencies with defined credentialing and typing roles under the NRF, NIPP, or NCPIP. The goal is an enhanced ability to manage assets during a national incident.

The elements of NIMS credentialing and typing are identification and qualification (roles, knowledge, skills, and abilities) for access control validation. DHS/FEMA requires identity and access control validation to be documented through the requirements of HSPD-12 and FIPS 201. The qualifications are typically defined based on a department or agency's roles within the ESF structure, CI Sector-Specific Agencies, or Government Coordinating Council.

Qualifications will be electronically assigned using FIPS 201 card and Identity Management System capabilities. Deployment authorization must be documented and may take several forms, from mission assignments to deployment orders and travel authorities. Until sufficient FIPS 201 card readers are available, separate paper copies of qualifications and deployment authorizations should be issued to FEROs so that the first three elements of NIMS credentialing and typing – identification, qualification/affiliation, and authority to deploy – can be inspected by access control personnel.

In addition to the requirements of this section, Federal agencies and FEROs must be familiar with the guidelines in Section 1.

IDENTIFICATION

Federal departments and agencies must comply with the requirements of HSPD-12/FIPS 201 to identify and designate employees and contractors. Federal departments and agencies must identify their personnel who are likely to be deployed in accordance with assignments in the NRF, NIPP, or NCPIP.[4] These personnel will be designated as FEROs and their FIPS 201 credentials visually marked accordingly.

QUALIFICATIONS

The qualifications of FEROs shall be determined by their department or agency based on the functions and missions these personnel will perform. They will be assigned to:

- The NRF ESF under which they will operate;
- The sector of the NIPP they will support; and/or

---

[4] Federal agencies are responsible for applying agency-specific inventory and qualification processes.

- Their national essential functions as government officials.

The FERO qualification must be electronically verifiable using the FIPS 201 credential. However, until card readers are universal, personnel must be issued qualification cards that can be visually inspected by access control officials.

DEPLOYMENT AUTHORIZATION

Each department and agency is responsible for providing FEROs with valid deployment authorization. Deployment under the Robert T. Stafford Disaster Relief and Emergency Assistance Act (42 § U.S.C. 5121 et seq.) occurs typically through the mission assignment process. For non-Stafford Act deployments or missions under a department or agency's statutory authority, it is clearly stated in the purpose section of the travel authorization.

While a mission assignment or travel authorization is acceptable at Federal facilities such as a Joint Field Office, it may be necessary to obtain supplemental documentation from State Emergency Operations Centers to validate the State's acceptance of the FEROs for access to State facilities or the disaster area.

DOCUMENTATION

The Post-Katrina Emergency Management Reform Act of 2006 (Pub. L. 109-295) requires each Federal department and agency to prepare an electronic inventory of all personnel determined to be FEROs, listing their assignment and the ESF or sector to which they are providing support upon activation. This inventory shall be submitted electronically to the FEMA Associate Administrator for Response and Recovery.

Each Federal department and agency provides periodic updates to the inventory. At a minimum, they must provide annual updates by May 1 to facilitate planning for hurricane season.

Section 3 – Guidance to State, Local, and Tribal Authorities and the Emergency Management Assistance Compact

GENERAL GUIDANCE

This section describes the characteristics recommended to State, local, and tribal authorities in adopting policies for credentialing response and recovery personnel deployed to an incident area.

APPLICABILITY

Compliance with the guideline is voluntary for non-Executive Branch Federal agencies. State, local, and tribal authorities are not required to credential their personnel in accordance with these guidelines. These entities do not need to comply with FIPS 201, the open technical standard used by Federal officials for uniform credentialing and access control or other Federal identification requirements for emergency response purposes. However, DHS strongly encourages State, local, and tribal authorities to use FIPS 201 and the PIV-I guidance in developing their credentialing systems.

A strong national preparedness and response system should be based on interoperability, commonality, and consistency. Therefore, DHS strongly recommends and requests that our partner governments build and implement a credentialing system consistent with these guidelines. DHS strongly recommends that the credentialing system developed incorporates the elements described herein to the maximum degree possible, should partner governments choose not to build a system completely compliant with the guideline.

IDENTIFICATION

State, local, and tribal authorities are encouraged to conduct identity enrollment of their personnel in accordance with GSA approved PIV-I. This level of vetting is essential even if these jurisdictions do not implement FIPS 201 or utilize the smartcard technology to ensure there is an appropriate level of trust in the identity of responder personnel.

QUALIFICATIONS

State, local, and tribal authorities should identify, type, and qualify their personnel in accordance with the published NIMS Job Titles.[5] For personnel that are not covered by the NIMS Job Titles, State, local, and tribal authorities should develop typing for these positions based on the essential functions of a position, levels of training, experience levels, required licensure and certifications, and physical and medical fitness for qualifying for the position.

---

[5] www.fema.gov/emergency/nims/ResourceMngmnt.shtml#item3.

CERTIFICATION

State, local, and tribal authorities should certify their personnel based on the completion of identity vetting and meeting the qualifications for the position to be filled.

BADGING

State, local, and tribal authorities should card their personnel after completing certification of their identity and qualifications and typing. Authorities are encouraged to utilize FIPS 201 and the PIV-I guidance for badging their personnel.

OTHER IMPORTANT ACTIVITIES

AUTHORIZATION AND ACCESS

As detailed in Section 1, being credentialed for identity and qualification is not authority for any person to self-deploy. Authorization for deployment may consist of order numbers, EMAC Request for Assistance (REQ-A), or travel authorizations with a stated purpose. Generally, persons that self-deploy without authorization should expect to be turned away from the disaster site. Additionally, the public safety personnel tasked with controlling access are responsible for denying access to unsafe or controlled areas by persons who are not credentialed or do not have proper authorization to deploy.

REVOCATION

As detailed in Section 1, State, local, and tribal authorities should ensure that personnel are credentialed only while they maintain their employment as well as currency in the qualifications for the position they hold. Upon termination of employment or affiliation, the authorities must revoke his or her credential and ensure that IT systems are updated within 18 hours.

NIMS-RELATED ACTIVITY GUIDANCE

PREPAREDNESS GRANTS

Federal agencies who make preparedness grants should allow State, local, and tribal governments to use these funds to implement the guideline, per NIMS Guide 0002. State agencies with devolved responsibility for awarding Federal preparedness grant funds to tribes should allow these funds to be used to implement the guideline, per NIMS Guide 0002. Nothing in this guideline requires any State, local, or tribal government to implement this guideline for mutual aid delivered exclusively within their jurisdictional borders.

EMERGENCY MANAGEMENT ASSISTANCE COMPACT

EMAC, established in 1996, is a congressionally ratified mutual aid agreement that provides form and structure to interstate mutual aid. All 50 States, the District of Columbia, Puerto Rico, Guam, and the U.S. Virgin Islands have enacted legislation to become EMAC members. States may also form other compacts that will have legal standing and jurisdiction if given the consent of the Congress. The Federal Government recognizes that EMAC may issue rules and adopt processes and services in addition to those mentioned in this guideline. Whenever EMAC is invoked, the following guidance applies:

- State and local officials provide support and assistance to ensure that a person deployed under EMAC can reach an appropriate incident check-in site or process;

- Unless otherwise directed by the incident/unified command, security and access controls should not unreasonably detain an individual deployed for mutual aid under EMAC. This guidance also applies to the accompanying team authorized to deploy with the individual (affiliate-access). If security and access control has the identity of the individual and the authenticity of the EMAC documentation, the responding individuals, team, and resources are to be processed and directed to reach check-in sites or processes as quickly as possible; and

- Unless the incident/unified command or the jurisdiction having authority establishes rules specific to the incident, disaster, or emergency, the identity of a person is established by documentation in the form of two government-issued photo IDs[6] or a photo ID and an official EMAC Request for Assistance Form (REQ-A) or an EMAC Mission Authorization Form (Mission Order).

---

[6] NIMS Guide 0002, NATIONAL CREDENTIALING DEFINITION AND CRITERIA, March 27, 2007

Section 4 – Model Standards and Guidance for Private Sector Organizations and Critical Infrastructure Owners and Operators

GENERAL GUIDANCE

Section 4 establishes the model standards for private sector entities and CI owners and operators in order to achieve timely response by appropriate CI responders. The private sector is not required to comply with the guideline, however, implementation and compliance with these recommendations ensures consistency with all credentialing activities by other response organizations and responder personnel.

APPLICABILITY

Compliance with the guideline is voluntary for non-Federal agencies. Private sector organizations and CI owners and operators do not need to conform their credentialing processes to FIPS 201, the open technical standard used by Federal officials for uniform credentialing and access control, or to other Federal identification requirements for emergency response purposes. However, DHS/FEMA encourages them to consider using FIPS 201 and the PIV-I guidance in developing their credentialing system.

A strong national preparedness and response system should be based on interoperability, commonality, and consistency. Therefore, DHS/FEMA recommends and requests that private sector organization and CI partners implement a credentialing process consistent with these guidelines. DHS/FEMA recommends that the credentialing system incorporate the elements described herein to the maximum degree possible, should private sector organizations and CI partners choose not to implement processes completely compliant with the guideline.

The purpose of this guideline is to facilitate access where feasible, not to mandate a one-size-fits-all approach. This guideline encourages incident commanders to establish access control based on just-in-time credentialing, accepting non-PIV or non-PIV-I credentials, or otherwise accommodating private sector and CI personnel.

IDENTIFICATION

Private sector entities and CI owners and operators are encouraged to conduct identity vetting of their personnel in accordance with the PIV-I guidance. This common practice is essential to facilitate interoperability even if they do not choose to implement FIPS 201 or utilize the smartcard technology to validate the identity of their employees.

QUALIFICATIONS

Private sector entities and CI owners and operators are encouraged to pre-identify, type, and qualify their emergency response employees in accordance with the published NIMS Job Titles.[7] For employees that are not covered by the NIMS Job Titles, private sector entities and CI owners and operators should use organizational and industrial standards for typing the positions and subsequent qualification of these employees.

For contracted personnel that are not employees of the company, the private sector companies should make every attempt to pre-identify any contractors who may potentially support restoration of private sector or CI operations.

CERTIFICATION

Private sector organizations, to include CI owners and operators, are encouraged to certify their employees based on the completion of identity vetting and meeting the qualifications of the position being filled.

BADGING

Private sector organizations and CI owners and operators are encouraged to card their personnel after completion of certification of their identity and qualifications and typing. Private sector organizations and CI owners and operators are encouraged to utilize PIV-I/FIPS 201 for badging their personnel. If they choose not to implement PIV-I/FIPS 201 electronic technology, the cards issued should conform to the visual elements of FIPS 201 as illustrated in Figure 1 in Section 1.

OTHER IMPORTANT ACTIVITIES

AUTHORIZATION AND ACCESS

As detailed in Section 1, being credentialed for identity and qualification/affiliation does not automatically serve as the authority for any person to self-deploy. Persons that self-deploy without authorization should expect to be turned away from the disaster site. Authorization for deployment can come from many sources that include a request from the incident commander, through a government emergency operation center, or from owners and operators of critical infrastructure. Owners and operators should follow procedures established by local jurisdictions for access to restricted incident areas. Additionally, the public safety personnel, under the incident commander, tasked with controlling access are responsible for establishing local access to unsafe or controlled areas.

---

[7] www.fema.gov/emergency/nims/ResourceMngmnt.shtm#item3

AFFILIATION ACCESS

Implementing an access control process to enable more rapid private-sector response and restoration efforts provides numerous benefits for overall incident management and response efforts. The three overarching goals of establishing an access control process for CI are:

- To enable CI owners and operators to restore their affected facilities quickly;
- To enable more rapid restoration of vital private sector economic activity; and
- To support the core NIMS principles of flexibility and standardization by encouraging State and local authorities to adopt a common approach to affiliation access for private-sector companies associated with any CI sector.

Affiliation-based access may be delayed until authorities determine that it is safe to enter the disaster site.

Access Control and Affiliation Documentation

Processes for access control and affiliation documentation should be administered by the States, tribes, or delegated to local authorities. The Incident Commander grants access to critical infrastructure owners and operators' facilities and services within an incident area and within a given timeline.

CI owners and operators are responsible for identifying the resources and personnel that will be deployed to repair, restore, and operate facilities. In addition, CI owners and operators will provide necessary documentation to deployed personnel. Finally, CI owners and operators will inform the authorities having jurisdiction of identified personnel and resources.

Implementation Guidance for Affiliation Access

The affiliation access process should:

- Ensure that appropriate authorities grant priority access to personnel, crews, and equipment needed for CI damage assessment and restoration before, during, and after an incident;
- Be easily communicated by government personnel to any CI or private sector requesting company to expedite their collaboration with the Incident Commander;
- Ensure that access decisions are communicated and recognized at all levels of access control;
- Enable processes that will support advance identification and authorization of CI entities, when practical. When affiliated personnel are not pre-credentialed public safety officials should work with the CI to expedite access. For example, it may be advisable to provide the appropriate affiliation documentation or credentials to certain known CI officials who will require access for damage assessments. However, it most likely is not possible to know in advance the full range of personnel and equipment that will be called in for CI facility or service repair and restoration; and

- Ensure that processes are consistent for State, local, tribal, and private-sector constituencies.

FEMA recommends that State, local, and tribal authorities consider the following actions in developing access control within their jurisdictions:

- Clearly define points of contact within State, local, and tribal governments, the ICS, and the private sector that have decision making responsibilities for access control, requests for information, and appeals for access;

- Support personnel and equipment access for corporate/company resources, as well as contractors who may be hired by CI owners and operators;

- Encourage pre-incident credentialing, typing, and documentation for CI;

- Provide for local discretion to expedite access and bypass requirements under certain conditions; and

- Participate in national, regional, State, local, and tribal exercises to ensure that emergency management at all levels, and CI within given jurisdictions, are aware of the program and begin to include it in their preparedness planning.

It is recommended that State, local, and tribal authorities consider the following for affiliation documentation within their jurisdictions:

- Allow for preapproval and registration for recognized CI within the jurisdiction to permit expedited access to an incident area if necessary;

- Allow authorized private sector and CI officials to distribute access control documents to response and recovery personnel/employees and contractors;

- Include provisions for news media personnel access as appropriate;

- Identify a centralized source for tags, invitation letters, or other affiliation documentation;

- Require responders to carry at least one form of government-issued photo identification;

- Allow admittance by large travel teams, such as convoys, with minimal delay;

- Allow for on-site distribution of access credentials for personnel already on scene; and

- Establish communication with local law enforcement, emergency response and recovery personnel, and all other Federal, State, local, and tribal agencies likely to respond to an incident.

REVOCATION

As detailed in Section 1, Private Sector and CI owners and operators should ensure that currently employed or contracted personnel are credentialed for purposes of affiliation access. Upon termination of employment or affiliation, the credentialing entity must revoke his or her card or other company-issued identification, and ensure that IT systems are updated appropriately. For entities wishing to comply with FIPS 201, the credentialing entity must ensure that IT systems are updated within 18 hours of revocation.

SECTION 5 – RECOMMENDATIONS FOR NONGOVERNMENTAL ORGANIZATIONS

GENERAL GUIDANCE

Section 5 establishes the recommended model credentialing standard for NGOs which collectively refers to voluntary, charitable, faith-based, and not-for-profit organizations. NGOs are not required to comply with these credentialing standards, however, their implementation and compliance with these recommendations ensures consistency with all credentialing activities by other response organizations and responder personnel.

APPLICABILITY

Compliance with the guideline is voluntary for non-Federal entities. NGOs are not required to credential their personnel in accordance with these guidelines or comply with FIPS 201, the open technical standard used by Federal officials for uniform credentialing and access control or other Federal identification requirements for emergency response purposes. However, DHS strongly encourages them to use FIPS 201 and the PIV-I guidance in developing their credentialing system.

A strong national preparedness and response system should be based on interoperability, commonality, and consistency. DHS therefore strongly recommends and requests that our partner governments, private sector organizations, and non-governmental organizations build and implement a credentialing system consistent with these guidelines. Should they choose not to build a system completely compliant with the guideline, DHS strongly recommends that the credentialing system developed incorporates the elements described herein to the maximum degree possible.

IDENTIFICATION

NGOs should conduct identity vetting of their personnel in accordance with PIV-I. This is essential even if they do not choose to implement FIPS 201 and utilize the smartcard technology to validate the identity of their employees and volunteers.

QUALIFICATIONS

NGOs should identify, type, and qualify their personnel and volunteers in accordance with the published NIMS Job Titles.[8] For personnel and volunteers that are not covered by the NIMS Job Titles, they should be qualified in accordance with the NGO standard for personnel and volunteers. The NGO should credential these personnel and volunteers based on identity and affiliation with the NGO being served.

---

[8] www.fema.gov/emergency/nims/ResourceMngmnt.shtm#item3

CERTIFICATION

NGOs should certify their personnel and volunteer employees based on the completion of identity vetting and meeting the qualifications of the position being filled or by simple affiliation with the NGO.

BADGING

NGOs should card their personnel only after they have certified their identity, as well as qualification/affiliation. NGOs are encouraged to utilize FIPS 201 for badging their personnel. If they choose not to implement FIPS 201 electronic technology, the cards issued should ideally conform to the visual elements of PIV-I and FIPS 201 as illustrated in Figure 1 in Section 1.

OTHER IMPORTANT ACTIVITIES

AUTHORIZATION AND ACCESS

As detailed in Section 1, being credentialed for identity and qualification/affiliation does not automatically serve as the authority for any person to self-deploy. Authorization for deployment may consist of a letter of invitation from an NGO in the disaster area. Generally, persons that self-deploy without authorization should expect to be turned away from the disaster site. Additionally, the public safety personnel tasked with controlling access are responsible for denying access to unsafe or controlled areas by persons who are not credentialed or do not have proper authorization to deploy.

Affiliation Access

For NGOs, it may not always be feasible or easy to confirm the qualifications of volunteers responding to an event. In this case, documented affiliation (identification) with a recognized NGO responding to the incident provides proof of authorization to deploy. Personnel in this category should be handled under Affiliation Access as recommended below.

Affiliation and Access Control Recommendations

Organizations are encouraged to seek the assistance of the respective State, tribal, and local governments to ensure consistency and compliance with their requirements and to integrate with the credentialing processes established in conformance with the guideline. Individuals who are officially requested, invited, authorized, credentialed, and typed are more likely to reach the emergency check-in points. State, local, and tribal governments may issue conforming credentials for the employees or volunteers of these organizations.

Adopting practices that work in concert with credentialing as defined in the guideline will integrate the organization's response/recovery personnel into the established incident command processes and facilitate critically needed response. To conform to the guideline, these organizations are encouraged to:

- Assist their personnel in obtaining and maintaining credentials that conform to the guideline;
- Ensure that individuals have proper identification in addition to a credential;
- Establish processes for responding to invitations/requests for assistance and for providing authorizations and documentation for their responders/response personnel;
- Maintain a roster or database of credentialed personnel to match the requests for interstate mutual aid with the resources and responders of the organization;
- Develop and maintain processes to assist government officials at receiving/security controls and check-in points to validate/verify identities, authorizations, and credentials; and
- Provide information to and training for their volunteers and employees about credentialing.

For those entities that will be using technology to enable credentialing, consider interoperability with FIPS 201 to allow for incorporation of common standards and a common trust framework.

Credentialing may be governed by State, local, and tribal laws. All organizations are encouraged to become familiar with these laws. Individuals who are not credentialed in accordance with these guidelines may be turned away on arrival at a disaster site. Furthermore, they may be subject to other actions by the proper authorities.

Nothing in this section or in NIMS Guide 0002 is to be interpreted to encourage, condone, or permit individuals to self-deploy, or to gain access to restricted areas during an emergency, or to hold immunities from tort and other liabilities that arise from their unauthorized actions.

REVOCATION

As detailed in Section 1, NGOs should ensure that personnel and volunteers are credentialed while they maintain their employment or affiliation with the NGO. Upon termination of employment or affiliation, the NGO must revoke his or her card and ensure that IT systems are updated appropriately. For entities wishing to comply with FIPS 201, the credentialing entity must ensure that IT systems are updated within 18 hours of revocation.

GLOSSARY OF TERMS AND DEFINITIONS

For the purposes of the NIMS Credentialing Guidelines, the following terms and definitions apply:

Access: As used in this document, the term "access" refers to the ability of a responder to gain entry to a disaster area.

Affiliate-access: This term refers to a type of access, used by individuals who are allowed access to a disaster because they accompany an otherwise authorized individual or entity. It primarily concerns utility repair crews, individuals volunteering through Non- Governmental Organizations, or persons associated with a Critical Infrastructure owner or operator. The process through which individuals qualify for access under this category is known as "affiliation access."

Affiliation access: This term refers to the procedures and systems devised by States and local authorities to permit utility repair crews, individuals volunteering through Non- Governmental Organizations, or persons associated with a Critical Infrastructure owner or operator to expedite the restoration of their facilities or provide services in areas affected by a disaster.

Check-in: The process through which resources first report to an incident. All responders, regardless of agency affiliation, must report in to receive an assignment in accordance with the procedures established by the Incident Commander. This term is not to be used to refer to security and access control situations.

Credentialed: Describes a person who has in his or her possession *all three* elements outlined in NIMS Guide 0002 (i.e., proof of (1) identity, (2) qualification or affiliation, and (3) authorization for deployment). Currently the three elements may be presented in physical and/or electronic format (e.g., hard-copy material or data transmitted using technologies). Any elements of credentialing established under EMAC, or under any State or tribal law for the specific intent of complying with this guideline, are to be used in the applicable jurisdiction.

Credentialing: The authentication and verification of the certification and identity of designated incident managers and emergency responders.

STATUTES

DHS/FEMA is issuing this guideline to comply with Section 510 of the Homeland Security Act of 2002, as amended (6 U.S.C. § 320). The guideline has been developed to establish definitions to explain and identify actions and processes that can provide the foundation for a consistent use and interoperability of credentialing on a national scale for the communities of interest defined herein. Its overall purpose is to strengthen NIMS and ICS to improve emergency management and response within the United States.

The Homeland Security Act, as amended, contains several sections to strengthen the use of ICS by establishing a credentialing guideline and guidance affecting Federal agencies and their authorized contractors to assist State, tribal, and local governments, and other emergency response official organizations. Nothing in this guideline is intended to displace or harm the mutual aid agreements that exist or arise within the United States or with its international mutual aid partners.

POINTS OF CONTACT

This guideline is issued by DHS/FEMA in accordance with the Homeland Security Act of 2002, as amended. For more information about this guideline or about credentialing under NIMS and ICS, contact: FEMA National Preparedness Directorate, National Integration Center at fema-nims@dhs.gov.

www.ingramcontent.com/pod-product-compliance
Lightning Source LLC
Chambersburg PA
CBHW080733290526
45790CB00008B/3181